Best wishes

Emma McL

:ö)

The Pet Detective Series

ARE GUINEA PIGS THE RIGHT PET FOR YOU?

Can *You* Find out the Facts?

5m Publishing

First published 2016

Copyright © Emma Milne 2016

Published by

5M Publishing Ltd,
Benchmark House, 8 Smithy Wood Drive, Sheffield, S35 1QN, UK

Tel: +44 (0) 1234 81 81 80
www.5mpublishing.com

A Catalogue record for this book is available from the British Library

ISBN 978-1-910455-11-1

Book layout by Mark Paterson
Printed by Bell and Bain Ltd, Scotland.
Photos by Dreamstime
Cover photos by Shutterstock

Pet Detectives: Guinea Pigs

Can You Find Out the Facts?

By

Emma Milne

BVSc MRCVS

For Alice and Charlotte.

Sorry I'm a better vet than I am a mum!
I love you all the way to the moon. And back.

Contents

Acknowledgements

This book would not have been possible without the fantastic support, photos and help from lots of people. A massive thank you to the wonderful Animal Welfare Foundation. Having endorsement from such a respected charity is a great privilege. Thank you to Emily Coultish for bringing my cartoon ideas to life and for putting up with my pedantry about details! Finally a huge thank you for granting use of their wonderful photos to David Perpiñán (DVM, MSc, Dip ECZM), Emma Keeble (BVSc, Diploma Zoological Medicine, RCVS Recognised Specialist in Zoo and Wildlife Medicine, MRCVS), Angela at C and C cages, RWAF, Rodrigo Conte, Niall Corbet, Tore Berg, Gary Kurtz and Paul B Jones. A very special mention also to Teresa Murphy of guineapigcagesstore.com and guineapigmarket.com for arranging a special photo shoot to show just how great guinea pig enclosures can be. I salute you all!

THE JOYS OF LIVING WITH ANIMALS.

Humans and animals have shared this lovely little planet of ours for thousands of years. Over that time we've used and needed animals in all sorts of different ways. First of all we needed their bodies and we used to use all the bits we could. We ate their meat and some of the other bits too like kidneys and livers and hearts. We got rich nutrients out of their bones in the bit called the marrow. We used their stomachs to carry water in or to cook other bits in. Animal fat was used to make oils and candles and fuel lamps and torches. Bones and horns could be made into tools and cups and we used their skins and fur to keep us warm and dry. Even things like a bison's tail could be made into anything from a fly swat to an ornament.

"Hey! I'm still using that!"

These days we still eat plenty of animals but we've found substitutes for some of the other bits. Over those thousands of years we started to realise that animals could be useful for other things. Cats were very good at catching mice and rats and other pests which ate our crops so having cats around started to look like a good thing. They could do jobs for us that we found hard. Wild dogs started creeping closer to human camps to get some warmth from our fires and steal scraps of our food. But in return humans got some protection from their natural guarding instincts and we learned that if we joined them in hunting we all made a pretty good team. Horses, donkeys and camels could be tamed and could carry big loads and cover distances which man couldn't even attempt. These animals are still used all over the world today.

As more time has gone by we've stopped needing animals so much to do things for us. We have cars and tractors, we have mouse traps and food containers that can't be chewed through, we have houses with alarms and strong doors and big locks and we have farmed animals to eat so we no longer need to hunt. But the simple truth is that we found out that animals are wonderful creatures and in the time we were getting to know each other humans started to fall in love with just having animals around.

THE JOYS OF LIVING WITH ANIMALS.

A dog putting its head on your lap to have his ears stroked gets some lovely affection but the human who's feeling those velvety ears and looking into those lovely brown eyes gets a lot back too. The cat stretched out on a warm rug by the fire has definitely 'landed on its feet' but the doting owner smiling in the doorway just watching the cat's tummy rise and fall with its breathing feels calm and happy without even realising it.

Pets make us happy. They make us feel calm and loved and wanted. Pets don't judge us or hold a grudge for days like your best friend did when you spoke to the new girl at school.

They are always there and they stick with you through thick and thin. In fact, sometimes they seem a lot nicer to be around than some humans!

The Serious Bit

The last point is the bit that is so important to remember; humans don't always do the right thing for their pets. Pets don't get to decide who buys them or how they are cared for. They have to live wherever you put them and they can only have the food you give them because they can't get to food themselves. When they go to sleep, how comfortable their bed is will be totally up to you. What you have to realise is that if you want a pet, those animals are *completely* dependent on you and your family to keep them happy, healthy and safe.

It sounds like an easy thing, doesn't it? Buy a cage, or a cat bed or a dog's squeaky toy, go to the pet shop and buy a bag of food and your pet will have everything it needs. WRONG! Thousands if not millions of pets have been kept this way and of course with food and water most animals can survive for years but that is just not enough. A great life isn't about coping or *managing* or *surviving*. It's about being HAPPY! If you were locked in your bedroom with no toys or books or friends or even your pesky sister you'd manage. As long as your mum gave you bread and stew twice a day and the odd bit of fruit you'd probably live for years. But would you be happy? It doesn't sound likely does it? You'd be bored out of your mind, lonely, miserable and longing for someone to play with, even if it was just that nose-picking sister or brother that you usually avoid like a fresh dog poo and make cry in front of your friends.

Having a pet, any pet, is a serious business. It's a bit like getting married or having a tattoo; you definitely shouldn't rush into it! You need to think carefully about lots of things. What sort of house or flat do you live in? How big is your garden if you have one? What other animals, if any, have you already got? How much money do your parents earn because I can tell you there is no such thing a cheap pet! How much spare time do you *actually* have? Are you an active family or a lazy one? All these questions have to be asked and they have to be answered very *honestly*. And of course you need to ask yourself what sort of animal do you want?

I've been a bit sneaky there because actually you should *never* ask yourself what sort of animal you want. You should think about what sort of animal you can look after properly. There's a very famous song from a long time ago called *You Can't Always Get What you Want* and I'm sure your mum or dad will have said it to you hundreds of times. You probably rolled your eyes, walked off in a huff, slammed a door and shouted 'THAT'S NOT FAIR!!' But I hate to say that your mum and dad are right and it's especially true when it comes to keeping pets. Lots of animals get abandoned or given away because people don't ask themselves the right questions, don't find out the facts and then, most importantly, don't answer the questions honestly.

Let's be honest, you lot are masters at pestering. For as long as children, parents and pets have been around, children have pestered, parents have caved in and pets have been bought on an impulse! This means without thinking and without knowing what the animal actually needs to be happy which usually means a very miserable pet.

But we're about to change all that aren't we? Because now I've got the dream team on my side. You chose to find out the facts about these animals so you *could* make the right choice. And I am very proud of you for that and I am very happy. So thank you.

The EVEN MORE serious bit!

So, you are thinking it would be nice to have a pet. You're certain you are going to love it, care for it, keep it happy and of course, NEVER get bored with looking after it and expect your mum and dad to do it. But what you need to know is that not only is that the right thing to do but it is also now the law. Sounds serious, doesn't it, but as I said, it's a serious business. In the United Kingdom in 2006 a new law was made called the Animal Welfare Act. This law says that anyone over the age of 16 looking after an animal has a 'duty of care' to provide for all the needs of the animal. Now laws are always written by people who use ridiculously long words and sentences that no-one else really understands but this law is very important to understand. A duty of care means it is the owner's responsibility to care for the animal properly and this law means that if the owner doesn't they could get their pet taken away and even, in rare cases, end up going to prison!

Aha, you may think if you live in the UK, I am not 16 so I'm fine and you'd be right, but the duty of care then falls to your mum or dad or whoever looks after

THE JOYS OF LIVING WITH ANIMALS.

you and the pet. So if you would like some guinea pigs, not only do you need to know all about them, you need to make sure the adults in the house do too. And you need to make sure they know about the law because they might not know what they are letting themselves in for!

If you don't live in the UK you need to find out what laws there are in your country about looking after animals. But remember, even if your country doesn't have any laws like this, making sure your animals are healthy *and* happy is still just the right thing to do.

Well, that's quite enough of all the boring serious stuff, let's learn some things about animals! The easiest way to find out about animals is to know about the five welfare needs. These apply to all pets, and in fact all animals, so they are good things to squeeze into that brilliant brain of yours so you can always remember them whenever you think about animals.

The Need for Fresh Water and the Right Food

This is a very obvious thing to say but you'd be surprised how many animals get given the wrong food. In fact, there was once a queen a very long time ago who wanted a zebra. I said wanted didn't I? She definitely didn't ask herself the right questions or find out the facts because when someone caught her one from the wild, she fed it steaks and tobacco!

Animals have evolved over a very long time to eat certain things and if they are fed the wrong foods they can get very ill, very fat, or miss vitamins and minerals they might need more than other animals. The right food in the right amounts is essential.

The Need for the Right Environment

This is a fancy way of saying where the animal lives. It could be a hutch, a cage, a house, bedding, shelter, a stable or lots of other things depending on the pet. It's very important that they are big enough, are clean, are safe and secure and the animals have freedom to move around.

The Need to Be With or Without Other Animals

Some animals live in groups and love to have company. Some animals are not very sociable at all, like me in the mornings! It's very important to know which your pet prefers. If you get it wrong you could have serious fighting and injuries or just a very lonely and miserable pet.

The Need to Express Normal Behaviour

Knowing what animals like to do is really important. As we said before lots of animals will survive on food and water but happiness or 'mental wellbeing' is just as important as being healthy or having 'physical wellbeing'. You've probably never thought about your own behavioural needs but imagine how you would feel if you were never allowed to go to the park or play or run or see your friends. You would soon be quite unhappy. Often you find that happy pets stay healthier, just like us.

The Need to Be Protected from Pain, Injury and Disease

Animals can get ill just like us and it will be up to you and your family to keep your pet healthy as well as happy. Just like you have vaccinations, they are very important for some animals to stop them getting ill and even dying. Animals, just like lots of children, also get worms, lice, mites and other parasites. You will need to find out how to treat or prevent these and look out for signs of them.

You need to check your animals over at least once a day to make sure there are no signs of problems and take them to a vet as soon as you think something is wrong. Vet costs are not cheap. You might also have a pet you can get health insurance for which is always a good idea.

So now you know the basic needs of all animals, it's time to concentrate on guinea pigs! Guinea pigs haven't actually been kept as pets for very long and still have lots of wild instincts and needs. The best way to learn what will keep your pet guinea pigs happy and healthy is to find out what guinea pigs in the wild are like. How do they live? What do they eat? Do they like to have others around and what makes them scared or nervous? In other words, what keeps them HAPPY? Shall we begin?

Chapter 2

GUINEA PIGS IN THE WILD.

People have been interested in guinea pigs for hundreds of years but maybe not for the same reasons that you are thinking about them now. Keeping animals as pets just because they are nice or cute is something that really never used to happen. In the olden days, and still in lots of countries, people had a tough time just keeping themselves and their children fed and healthy. The only reason they kept animals was to eat or to help them with jobs like farming.

We might think it's terrible to eat a little cutie like a guinea pig but they have helped feed people for hundreds of years and they are still a very important source of meat today.

GUINEA PIG FACT

Roughly 65 MILLION guinea pigs are still eaten every year just in Peru. That's about the same number as there are people living in the UK! The people in Peru think that guinea pigs are so brilliant that they have festivals devoted to them.

As well as being nice with some roast potatoes these rather unfortunate animals were also used for some of the earliest medical experiments. Guinea pigs get some of the same diseases as humans so doctors have used them to try to find out why humans get poorly and how we can cure these diseases. That's why now if people are used in an experiment they are called guinea pigs!

GUINEA PIG FACT

Some witch doctors used to use guinea pigs to tell them what was wrong with people. They believed that if you rubbed a guinea pig on a sick person's body the pig would tell you what the disease was! Supposedly black guinea pigs were especially good at it!

"Don't worry. You'll feel right as rain in a minute!"

A beautiful wild guinea pig

The guinea pigs we keep as pets are very close relatives of these wild pigs and still have all the same instincts, needs and fears. One of the most important things to know about any animal to help you understand what makes them happy or scared is whether they are a prey animal or a predator. Let me explain...

Over the millions of years that there has been life on our beautiful planet, plants and animals have grown and evolved together in a delicate balance, all linked together by the food they eat. Some animals eat plants, some, like humans and bears, eat plants *and* animals and some just eat other animals. These relationships are called food chains. For guinea pigs one food chain might go like this;

That's enough about what humans think of guinea pigs, let's find out about how wild guinea pigs live. Imagining wild guinea pigs seems a bit funny doesn't it but there are still lots of guinea pigs living free in the wild just like rats, mice and rabbits.

GUINEA PIG FACT

They are not from Guinea at all but come from South America. No one is really sure how they got their name. They are also called cavies. Wild guinea pigs still live in South America in countries like Peru, Brazil and Ecuador.

The guinea pig eats the grass and the snake eats the guinea pig. Prey animals are ones which are eaten and predators are the ones which eat the other animals. In the case of our food chain above, the guinea pig is the prey because it is eaten by the snake. The snake is the predator because it eats the guinea pig. Of course lots of animals are both predator and prey if you think about it. For example, tuna are huge fish which live in the oceans and eat smaller fish so they are predators. But then a human comes along, catches the tuna and eats it in a big sandwich with some mayonnaise and sweetcorn. The tuna is the prey and the human is the predator.

GUINEA PIGS IN THE WILD.

By the way, if you tried to fit the biggest tuna fish in a sandwich it would be roughly the same size *and weight* as a small car!

So now we know that guinea pigs are prey animals and this is really important because it explains lots about the way they live, how they behave and what makes them feel happy, safe and secure. I think it's good sometimes to think about how you might feel in certain similar situations. By finding out how animals live naturally you can compare it to things in your life and it helps you to empathise with your pets. This means imagine how they might be feeling. You'll see what I mean as we go along.

Imagine how you feel when you're frightened. Think about some of those scary dreams we all have where you wake up in the night and you're absolutely petrified. Something scary in your dream was chasing you and you couldn't quite get away. Your heart is pounding, your mouth is dry, you're all sweaty and it takes a few minutes to realise it was just a dream, you're safe at home and the only thing threatening you is the awful smell of foot fungus and wind wafting over from your smelly brother!

That scared feeling and all the things that go with it like the racing heart are because of something your body makes called adrenaline. It's an amazing hormone, released in an instant whenever an animal (or a human) feels threatened. It's often called the fight or flight hormone. In the wild for animals to survive they either need to stand their ground and fight or, usually more sensibly, RUN AWAY!

Nowadays humans don't often need to run away from a lion or a bear but adrenaline still kicks in in plenty of other scary situations; at exam time, when you have to walk past the school bully, when you're taking the all important penalty shot that could win the game and of course, when your mum shouts for you and uses your *middle* name. You know you're in trouble then.

Now imagine being a prey animal. Those chasing dreams aren't just dreams; they're things you have to look out for every single minute of every single day. Prey animals have various ways of avoiding being eaten depending on what sort of animal they are, where they live and also on what sort of animal is trying to eat them. Some use camouflage, some play dead while some are quick runners.

© Paul B Jones
RUN AWAY! Always a good defence!

Some have fearsome defences like horns and some, like the skunk, just smell *really* bad! But lots of prey animals like guinea pigs use the form of defence that human armies use and that is strength and safety in numbers.

Living in a group has lots of advantages. There are more eyes and ears on the lookout for danger. With more lookouts everyone gets more time to eat, play and groom. Moving as a group can confuse predators because they suddenly forget which one of you they were after in all the chaos. And, quite selfishly, any one animal in the group is less likely to be eaten the more animals there are around it. Think back to your 'adrenaline rush' at the sight of the school bully. Would you rather go past him (or her!) alone or with a group of your friends? Sometimes we all need a little moral support.

Guinea pigs in the wild live in groups of about ten adults and their babies. Just like actual pigs the males are called boars and the females are called sows. Just to be different though the babies are called pups, like seals. The group usually has one boar and the rest of the adults are sows. Guinea pigs don't have big powerful legs like rabbits so they can't dig their own burrows to live in to stay safe from predators. They tend to hide out in dips and crevices and under plants. They also sometimes get a bit cheeky and move in to burrows that other animals have already dug.

© Tore Berg
Dangly plants make a good hiding place

GUINEA PIG FACT

Groups of guinea pigs are called herds, like cows, and, like cows, sometimes when they are startled or scared they stampede in all directions to confuse predators.

"STAMPEDE!"

GUINEA PIGS IN THE WILD.

The most obvious way that wild guinea pigs differ from our pets is their colour. We've bred guinea pigs to be all sorts of beautiful colours and patterns. In the wild they are various shades of brown. I'm sure you can imagine that being bright orange and white wouldn't help you hide in a background of grass and mud in the wild!

© Tore Berg

Spot the difference!

As well as being mud coloured and living in groups, wild guinea pigs have more ways to avoid predators. Like lots of prey animals they come out at dusk and dawn. Lots of predators rely on good light to see their prey. By grazing at dusk and dawn guinea pigs are much harder to spot. You might have heard of the word 'nocturnal' for animals which are out and about at night, well the word for animals like guinea pigs is 'crepuscular'.

Communication between members of a group is very important. There's not much point looking out for predators for each other if you can't tell the others when you see one. Animals communicate in different ways and guinea pigs are really chatty creatures. They have lots and lots of different noises they make which all mean different things. They have greeting wheeks, warning rumbles, excited chattering and all sorts of squeaks in between and they quickly call to each other if there is danger coming. If you do get some guinea pigs as pets you'll soon start to learn their language and know when they are excited to see you.

Prey animals in the wild are most in danger when they are babies or very young. Lots of animals that live in holes or burrows like rabbits or mice have babies that are blind, have no fur and can't care for themselves at all. They tuck them away in their little nests far underground where they are as safe as possible while they grow. Guinea pigs can't do this because they spend most of their time just hiding away in natural cubbyholes. This means their babies have to be raring to go when they come out. Guinea pig babies are born like perfect miniatures of their mums and dads, eyes open, fully furred and able to eat solids almost as soon as they are born. The term for babies like this is 'precocious'. Not only does this mean they can fend for themselves straight away it also means they are SUPER cute! Just so you know, if someone calls you a precocious brat it usually doesn't mean they think *you* are being super cute!

To get babies this well developed a guinea pig pregnancy is as long as a dog's. That's about 63 days! By the end of it the mother is bulging and you can see the babies wriggling around inside her.

A common difference between prey animals and predators is their eyes. Predators usually need very accurate eyesight to fix their prey and judge how far away they are. The best place to have eyes to do this is on the front of your face, pointing forwards, like humans, dogs and cats. Prey animals don't need accurate vision but they do need to see what's coming from every direction, including birds of prey from the sky. The best place to have eyes that see everywhere is on the side of your head.

Guinea pigs can see almost everything behind them, above them and in front of them without moving their heads. A bit like teachers.

© Gary Kurtz

Eyes on the side of your head let you see in all directions

© Niall Corbet

So, guinea pigs sleep most of the day and then they creep out at dusk, they have a good look round for predators and then what? They EAT! The main thing that wild guinea pigs eat is grass.

Grass and similar plants are hard to grind up and even harder to digest so animals which live on these foods have had to evolve ways to get at the goodness locked inside those woody leaves. Firstly they need really good teeth.

© Rodrigo Conte

Guinea pigs forage around for sprouts of fresh grass on the dry plains.

© Niall Corbet

GUINEA PIGS IN THE WILD.

Guinea pigs are rodents like rats and mice and have very sharp incisor teeth like little chisels. The incisor teeth snip through the plants like garden shears and then the food is pushed to the molar teeth at the back to be ground up. One very important thing to know about guinea pig teeth is that they never stop growing through their whole life. This is because grass and plants need to be smashed and ground really well before being swallowed. These foods don't contain many nutrients so animals living on them need to eat A LOT to get everything they need. This means guinea pigs have to spend most of the time they are awake grazing and all that grinding wears teeth down pretty quickly. This is why their teeth must keep on growing or they would soon disappear altogether!

Now I'm going to tell you something about guinea pigs that is going to make you very glad you're a human and not a guinea pig. There is something else they eat besides grass and other plants. Their own POO! That's right, the way guinea pigs get all the nutrients out of their tough diet is by eating it twice. Eating poo is called coprophagy and for guinea pigs it's simply essential. When guinea pigs are resting they produce soft, sticky poo called caecotrophs which is covered in mucus a bit like snot. The guinea pig eats this snotty poo straight out of its own bottom. Yum! The mucus protects the poo from all the strong acids and juices in the stomach and then when it gets further down the intestines it is digested a second time and all the vitamins, minerals and goodness get a second chance to be absorbed.

"eat up then, darling"

GUINEA PIG FACT

When guinea pigs are really happy or excited they do something called 'popcorning' where they jump up and down repeatedly in happy little hops. Boing!

So now you know pretty much everything there is to know about guinea pigs in the wild, we better get down to the tricky business of keeping them as happy, healthy pets.

Chapter 3

We've already said that having a great life is what we should try to give all our pets and the best start to that is to get the basic survival stuff exactly right from the very start. The top three things needed for life are air, water and food. Animals, including humans, can't live without these things and when it comes to food, getting the right diet and feeding the right *amounts* of food will get your guinea pigs off to a brilliant start for a healthy and happy life.

Let's tackle the easy part first. Water. Water is absolutely essential for every living thing on Earth. For animals like humans and guinea pigs after the need for air, water is the most important thing. If animals can't get to enough water they can get very ill and die really quickly. Water is the only thing your guinea pigs need to have to drink. Depending on the food you give them they will also get some water in their food, say for instance, in some juicy grass, but it's essential they have access to plenty of fresh water all the time as well. Just like us they will need to drink more during warm weather compared to cold weather and also if they've been very active, running, exploring and playing.

Lots of you will have seen the water bottles that most small animals have attached to the sides of their cages. These are fine but it's very important that you check them at least twice a day because the little balls that let the water flow out of the nozzles can get stuck. If this happens it might look like your guinea pigs have plenty of clean water but they actually can't get to it! This would be very frustrating for them but is also very dangerous because water is vital for life. It's best to offer one or two bowls of water as well. If you think back to our wild guinea pigs they are never going to drink water out of a bottle are they? They will sip from puddles, streams and lakes depending on where they live. Guinea pigs are creatures of habit and don't like change so make sure you know what they were used to drinking out of where you got them from. If you use bowls talk to the people at the shop about which bowls are best and not likely to tip over and make everything cold and wet.

However you are giving water, just as with the bottles you need to check the water at least twice a day. Make sure it is clean and there is plenty available. Bowls can end up with bedding and food in them so need to be cleaned every day, and, if they're dirty again, twice a day. Bottles might keep water clean for longer but it's still important to check them twice a day to make sure the water is flowing. You still need to change the water in the bottles every day even if it looks clean because it can get stale or get algae growing in it which can make your guinea pigs poorly.

Some guinea pigs will find drinking from a bowl much more natural.

FRESH WATER AND THE RIGHT FOOD.

So, first we need air, then water and then of course we need food. Bodies are amazing machines and make any computer or machine that humans have built look like the most ridiculously rubbish toy imaginable. Like all machines, bodies need energy to make them work. Because our bodies are so spectacularly clever they can also fix themselves and replace their own parts. Instead of plastic and metal bits or replacement batteries they need vitamins and minerals, fibre, proteins, fats and carbohydrates. All animals get these from their food and over the millions of years that

© Niall Corbet

Wild guinea pigs have evolved to get all the goodness from grass and leafy plants.

animals have been on the planet they have evolved different ways to get all the things they need from their foods. As we said about wild guinea pigs they eat lots of plants that don't have much goodness in any one bit. This means they have to eat lots of it, they need to chew it really well and in the case of guinea pigs, just like rabbits, they eat it twice to make sure they get every scrap of goodness out of it.

Now it might surprise you to know that guinea pigs are just like humans in more ways than one when it comes to food. We both need all the food groups like fibre and protein that we mentioned before but we also both have a very special need when it comes to vitamin C. Vitamin C is essential for keeping you healthy. There are plenty of animals that can make their own vitamin C from other foods but humans, guinea pigs and some other animals like bats can't do that because we don't have the right tools to make it. This means we simply must get the vitamin in our food. Luckily for us it's found in all sorts of gorgeous fruits and vegetables so there's plenty of it if you eat the right things.

If we, and all those other animals, don't get enough vitamin C we get a very serious disease called scurvy. When humans first started exploring the world hundreds of years ago we didn't know all these clever things about how our bodies work. Sailors stocked up on lots of food to take on their long voyages but fruit and vegetables go rotten very quickly so they didn't last long into the journey. The sailors' bodies soon ran out of vitamin C and scurvy was very common. It caused the deaths of hundreds of sailors (and plenty of pirates too) until we found out what was needed to prevent it. That's why it's so important to eat your fruit and veg, especially if you want to be an explorer!

In guinea pigs scurvy causes weakness, bleeding, bad gums and skin problems among other things and will kill them if not treated. In the wild, guinea pigs nibble lots of different leafy plants. This variety, along with their main food, grass, makes sure they get all the vitamin C they need. As you'll see, a good variety of the right foods for your pet guinea pigs is also important.

As I said before, nature is very clever at balancing things and keeping everything happy and it's usually humans that make a mess of it. This is what happened when we started keeping guinea pigs as pets. We thought it would be much easier and better for them if we made them some nice easy food to eat instead of all that rubbish grass. They could get all their nutrients out of a convenient bowl in easy to eat cereals pieces, a bit like muesli that some people have for breakfast. No need for much of that boring grass or hay. Do you remember the danger of assuming animals are like humans? Exactly. Animals like guinea pigs *love* eating grass and hay and plants. That's what they spend most of their time awake doing. Their teeth never stop growing so they absolutely *have* to keep chewing and chewing to keep their teeth healthy. Overgrown teeth can be disastrous for guinea pigs, cause pain and abscesses full of pus in their mouths and even kill them. So our old idea of a good diet for them wasn't so good after all.

© PDSA

Muesli should NOT be fed to your guinea pigs.

Giving guinea pigs muesli style food is like you being given a bowl of cabbage, bread, beans, Brussels sprouts and sweets all mixed together for all your meals. There are things in there that would definitely get left! Guinea pigs, just like humans, pick out their favourite bits, which means they don't have a balanced diet and might not get some of the vitamins and minerals they need.

The food crumbles easily as well so they don't spend enough time chewing to keep their teeth healthy and can end up having pain, lots of trips to the vet, and even sometimes being put to sleep. On top of this lots of them get way too fat. This happens partly because sometimes people give them more food than they need but also because they're used to eating food that's a bit rubbish! Their bodies have evolved to be experts at getting every scrap of goodness out of their food. So when humans come along and give them food full of energy in small parcels they can easily get way too fat.

Being too fat, or obesity as it is called, is a real problem for animals and humans alike. You don't find fat animals in nature. Some animals will build up stores of fat to keep them warm and give them energy through the winter but you will never find a truly fat animal in the wild. Being too fat can give lots of animals diseases and the extra weight puts strains on joints and bones and gives the heart too much work to do. You can imagine that a fat prey animal might struggle to get away from a predator and wouldn't live long enough to have fat babies. This really is survival of the fittest!

"Well, this is going to be easy!"

Chapter 3

Being overweight can also make it very hard to keep clean. Lots of animals need to groom themselves to stay clean and keep their fur and skin healthy. Being too fat makes this really hard and for guinea pigs especially this is a big problem. We'll look at these problems more in Chapter 7 but for now all we need to know is that the right diet and the right amount of food is really important.

Pellet food stops selective feeding.

So, muesli is out of the window for guinea pigs. (It can be really good for humans though so if your mum insists you eat it for breakfast I can't help you there!). These days we still give guinea pigs a little bit of dry 'complete' food but it's best to buy pellets, NOT muesli. Pellets are made in a way that doesn't let the guinea pigs pick and choose which bits they like and makes sure they get everything they need. It's very important to make sure you buy guinea pig pellets not food for other pets like rabbits. Guinea pig pellets have extra vitamin C added to them.

You also need to be careful about what hay you give and what kind is in your pellets. One type of hay called Alfalfa has lots of a mineral called calcium in it. This is good for very young, growing guinea pigs and pregnant ones but not for normal adults. Too much calcium goes through them into their wee and can build stones in their bladders. For adult guinea pigs, get pellets made of grass hay or Timothy hay. Maybe you could call one of your pigs Timothy and then you'll always remember! It all sounds a bit complicated doesn't it but don't worry, we'll make sure they get plenty of vitamin C from other food too.

Things you need to know about this pesky vitamin is that not only do we really need it but it doesn't last very long and it disappears even more quickly when exposed to air and light. This means that by the time you get to the end of a big bag of pellets there might not be any vitamin C left! Always buy small bags, check that they have a 'useby' date on them and keep them tightly closed in a dark place when you get them home. Try not to leave heaps of pellets sitting in your guinea pigs' bowl. Pellets should be the smallest part of their diet so just offer about an eggcup full each once a day. If it all gets eaten you can always add more later but don't just top bowls up or some bits might have lost their vitamin C.

Most importantly just like their wild relatives your guinea pigs need lots of what's called long fibre foods to keep their teeth and guts healthy and that means fresh grass and good quality hay.

© RWAF

Hanging baskets make great hay racks.

Always make sure hay is given in a hay rack or something similar to keep it clean.

Just having hay as bedding isn't good enough because it could be too wet and dirty for the guinea pigs to eat. If you're planning to keep them outside and they'll have safe access to grass all the time then don't worry too much, they won't go hungry, just make sure hay is always there if they want it. Sometimes they might not feel like going outside if they are frightened or if the weather's horrible and if they always have hay they can choose what they want to do. If you've guinea pigproofed your garden you need to make sure you know which plants you have growing there that the guinea pigs might get to. This is important because some plants can be very poisonous.

If your guinea pigs will be allowed to explore you need to know what plants they might find...

...and of course you could make sure there are some nice ones to find!

Fresh grass is lovely for guinea pigs and if yours are indoors you can pick fresh grass for them. Don't give them clippings from the lawnmower though. These can go off very quickly and make your guinea pigs ill.

So hay or grass should always be available no matter where you keep your guinea pigs. Now let's talk about that lovely variety of other things they might like. Guinea pigs are a bit like toddlers in a way because they decide what foods they like and they sometimes don't like trying new things! This is why it's important to get them used to a good variety early on. Whenever you offer them something new offer a little bit at a time and increase the amounts slowly. This way they'll get used to new foods without getting an upset tummy.

There are lots of leafy vegetables that guinea pigs love and remember you'll want some that have lots of vitamin C in them too. Broccoli, carrot tops, salad peppers, kale, spinach and tomatoes are all safe but there are lots more too. You'll be finding out all about those later. Never feed them potatoes, potato tops, rhubarb, or tomato leaves as these are poisonous.

FRESH WATER AND THE RIGHT FOOD.

Guinea pigs also love various fruits because they are sweet but this can be a problem. Fruits are the guinea pig equivalent of a pick 'n' mix; high in sugar and irresistible! They can make your guinea pigs fat and cause tooth problems so should be a very occasional treat at the most. Things like strawberries, kiwi fruit and apple are usually popular.

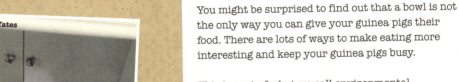

© Liz Yates

You need to watch out though because, also like toddlers, they sometimes help themselves!

© Liz Yates

You might be surprised to find out that a bowl is not the only way you can give your guinea pigs their food. There are lots of ways to make eating more interesting and keep your guinea pigs busy.

This is part of what we call environmental enrichment. It's a bit like you having posters on your wall, books to read or a TV rather than a blank, white box for a bedroom! So now we better look at the type of 'environment' that keeps guinea pigs happy and healthy as well as how we can 'enrich' it or make it even better.

Sometimes a bowl causes a bit of a jam!

THE NEED FOR THE RIGHT ENVIRONMENT.

Repeat after me a thousand times:

'A HUTCH IS NOT ENOUGH!'

Well, that was a short chapter, wasn't it?

On second thoughts maybe we *should* say a little more than that. You may have heard this expression about rabbits but just the same is true when it comes to guinea pigs.

A long time ago when humans started keeping guinea pigs they were not being kept because they were cute pets. They were being kept to be eaten. In those days most people didn't really care very much about animal happiness, they just needed the animals to survive long enough to get fat enough to go on a plate! The easiest way to keep guinea pigs was in cages and the smaller the better so they didn't take up too much room. The same is still true today in some of the countries where guinea pigs are farmed for food. Unfortunately, when guinea pigs started becoming pets instead of dinner no one really thought to change the cages.

This means that for years and years people have assumed that guinea pigs don't need much room at all, can sit in a hutch or a cage all day on their own being fed muesli and will be perfectly happy. Actually what it's meant is that thousands, maybe hundreds of thousands, of guinea pigs have had the most miserable, boring, lonely and sometimes painful lives imaginable. So how do we work out what might make our pet guinea pigs happier? That's right! Look to the wild.

It can be a big and scary world from a guinea pig's point of view!

THE NEED FOR THE RIGHT ENVIRONMENT.

As we said, wild guinea pigs live in close-knit groups and hide in dips and holes and vegetation. They are prey animals so they want to feel like they can hide whenever they get worried about predators. They like to be near each other so they can chatter and stay in touch. But they also always have room to get away from each other if one of the others is being annoying or a bully. When the guinea pigs choose to come out in the open they can run, explore, graze, groom, popcorn and PLAY! So if you were thinking that guinea pigs don't need much room it's time to think again.

Guinea pigs can be kept indoors or outdoors depending on how big your garden or house is, what the weather is like most of the time where you live and also how house-proud your grown-ups are! If there's one thing for sure it is that guinea pigs are very messy creatures. The space they need will be similar inside and out but the hutches will vary from the indoor cages so we'll talk about both options.

Outdoor Living

The first thing to remember is that the hutch should never be the only place your guinea pigs have to live. It should be somewhere they can shelter in bad weather or hide away from things they are afraid of and they definitely need to be able to get in and out of it whenever they want to. When they choose to be in there they need to be able to stretch out full length to relax, stand up to explore the hutch and have enough room to escape each other if they need to as well.

Your guinea pigs will also need room for their food, water, toilet area and their sleeping area. All this added together means that the *smallest* hutch you should ever consider buying needs to be at least 1.2 metres long, at least 70cm wide and at least 50cm high. If you're thinking about having a group and not just a pair it will need to be even bigger. Quite often in life you'll hear people say that size doesn't matter but when it comes to hutches it definitely does matter! The bigger you can afford the better. In fact, some people even use a garden shed which can make brilliant-sized guinea pig houses.

© RWAF

Sheds make big luxury hutches

If you do decide to use the shed remember that they can get really hot so your family will need to make sure there is plenty of ventilation, especially in the summer. Of course with any housing the opposite is also true and your hutch will need to be protected from the worst of the weather as well as the sunshine. Rain often has a favourite direction so try and work out what that is wherever you live and make sure your hutch is sheltered from it. Guinea pigs don't cope well with extremes of temperature or draughts so you need to try and make sure their environment stays as sheltered and consistent as possible and the hutch will have to be raised off the ground.

There are all sorts of bedding that you can buy but some like sawdust and wood shavings can make your guinea pigs poorly, and simple, shredded paper gets quickly wet and isn't very good. It's probably best not to use straw as bedding either because guinea pigs can sometimes scratch the surface of their eyes on stiff bedding like straw.

In winter or in cold spells you'll need to move your hutch inside. You can move it into a shed if you have one or into the garage but you'll need to leave the car outside in case the fumes make your guinea pigs ill. And remember that wherever they are they'll still need to be able to come and go into their exercise area.

Stick to plenty of dust-free hay or the newer processed paper and wood pulp products to be on the safe side. The sleeping area will need lots of nice deep bedding like hay. All the bedding will need checking every day so you can take out the smelly or dirty bits. You need to top up the cosy bits, especially in winter, and if you're using edible bedding like hay. At least once a week, all of the bedding should be changed.

THE NEED FOR THE RIGHT ENVIRONMENT.

So now you have a huge hutch or a shed which is practically a guinea pig palace and next you'll need an exercise run for them. A mistake that lots of people make is to have a run that is separate from the hutch. They take the guinea pigs out of the hutch, carry them to the run and put them in there for however long they are at work or think the guinea pigs might like to be there. But how do we know what the guinea pigs want to do? We can't read minds. If you were in the living room and your mum was insisting on 'just quickly watching the news headlines' you might decide to go in the garden or sit in your bedroom and read a fantastic pet care book. Whatever you do would be your choice and our pets need to have choice too. Guinea pigs need to be able to come and go from the hutch whenever they want to.

Imagine if you left them in a separate run and went out for hours. It could tip down with rain or a big hungry cat might be lurking about scaring the guinea pigs out of their wits. With freedom of choice they can feel safe and secure and sheltered whenever they need to or explore and play when the fancy takes them.

The other problem with the carrying back and forth to a run which might surprise you is that guinea pigs don't actually like being picked up and carried about. Remember they are prey animals and they like to know they are close to the ground and able to bolt to safety at the drop of a hat. Being picked up feels like being carried away by a bird of prey. They don't understand you are there to look after them and you are their friend. When you first get them they might even think you are a predator, and with some humans they'd be right! So picking them up and carrying them around should be avoided as much as possible because it can make them really frightened. If they're frightened they are more likely to struggle and scramble to get away. This makes them difficult to hold and if you dropped them they could get badly injured. All in all it's best to leave them on the floor as much as you can and when you do handle them make sure you're sitting down and they can't fall. If you were after a pet that was guaranteed to like a cuddle then guinea pigs might not be the ones for you. It takes a lot of time, patience and effort to gain the trust and affection of pet guinea pigs.

With this in mind the best thing to do is have a run that is always attached to their hutch. This could mean the hutch sits inside a big run or you could have a tunnel or doorway connecting the two. The main thing is that the guinea pigs can always choose where they want to be. There are lots of accessories you can buy to link different areas safely together so you can always keep adding bits on to keep them entertained and interested and give them new places to explore.

The smallest exercise area should be at about three metres long and at least two metres wide but just the same as we said with the hutch, the bigger the better.

© RWAF
You can use tunnels to join the hutch and run.

Constant access to grass lets guinea pigs graze as they would in the wild.

The run needs to have shade and protection on at least part of it so that your guinea pigs can be outside and graze even if the sun is strong or it's raining. A thick tarpaulin tied over a portion of the run works well for both these situations and should be fairly easy to get hold of.

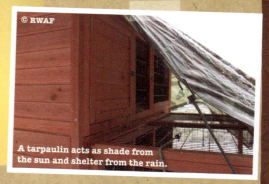
© RWAF
A tarpaulin acts as shade from the sun and shelter from the rain.

THE NEED FOR THE RIGHT ENVIRONMENT.

Indoor Living

If you're thinking about turning your palace into your guinea pigs' palace there's one thing you absolutely have to do. CHECK WITH YOUR MUM AND DAD! I know that being the amazing, responsible pet detectives you are, you are going to check all of this with your family but guinea pigs can make a lot of mess and cause some damage so it's really important. When you Google guinea pig cages you will get a massive choice of small and pathetic cages! We are going to change the world of guinea pig keeping, you and I. The minimum cage size is still the same indoors as your outdoor hutch, that is 1.2m x 70cm x 50cm. But remember this is the absolute minimum and the bigger you can manage the better. If you do have this size they will still need either constant access to a bigger exercise area or you'll need to make sure they get let out in a safe area for plenty of 'floor time'. Make sure the cages do not have wire floors because this can cause very painful damage to your guinea pigs' feet. Don't use glass tanks like fish tanks either because they are way too small but also don't let enough air circulate and can make your pigs really poorly.

There are some brilliant cage designs these days where you can make almost any combination of sizes and levels and be really inventive.

You can start with this...

...and turn it into something like this!

This way you can make a giant cage so that they can exercise and explore as and when they want to. The more space your guinea pigs have the happier and healthier they will be. When you're thinking about where to put your cage remember that guinea pigs are naturally timid prey animals. Make sure they are in a quiet room away from the hustle and bustle of your life and especially any dogs or cats you might have. The room will also need to be a consistent temperature, not somewhere like a conservatory which will get very hot and very cold.

sometimes the smallest things TAKE UP THE MOST ROOM IN YOUR HEART

A quiet bedroom away from a radiator is ideal.

© C and C cages

You can use hay for bedding indoors...

Bedding will be the same indoors as outdoors but some people also buy fleecy bedding or use towels for indoor guinea pigs now. You'll need to check with your mum or dad before you do this though because I'm guessing it might be them doing all the washing!

© Cagetopia™

...or fleecy linings and cushions

Let's talk about floor time, when your pigs are going to get to explore. This can be great exercise and stimulation for your pigs and also lovely time for you to spend watching them. BUT you need to remember some things. Firstly they have sharp, chisel teeth. Whenever your guinea pigs are out of their cage they can chew carpets, cupboards, sofas and tables as well as anything else they fancy. More important than the damage they could do to your house you need to remember how dangerous your house could be for them! Every electrical wire will need to be out of reach or covered so they can't be chewed because an electric shock will easily kill them.

THE NEED FOR THE RIGHT ENVIRONMENT.

© Liz Yates

Your pigs won't know what is meant for them to eat and what isn't so watch out!

You'll also need to make sure all your house plants are well and truly out of reach. There are so many different types of plants kept in houses these days it's almost impossible to know which are safe to eat. Best to be safe and keep them all out of the way.

You also need to know that guinea pigs can squeeze into TINY places so wherever you let them out make sure you'll be able to safely get them back.

Right back at the end of the last chapter we mentioned something called 'environmental enrichment'. Now we've learnt about the right sorts of environment for pet guinea pigs it's time to look at how to enrich it. Just as it sounds, this means to make it even better. We said right at the start that happiness is just as important as being healthy and that is what I'd love you to ALWAYS remember when it comes to pets. A big hutch or cage is nice, like you having a comfy house to live in, but if you couldn't do fun things and see your friends as well you wouldn't be *happy*. Well guinea pigs are just the same and the next two needs are virtually impossible to look at separately. You'll see why as we go along.

In the meantime if there's one thing you remember from this chapter make sure it's this:

A HUTCH IS NOT ENOUGH!!!!

THE NEED TO BE WITH OR WITHOUT OTHER ANIMALS.

All the needs of animals are important but for many animals this is probably the *most* important one for being happy so we need to get it right. You might have noticed that so far I've only used the word 'guinea pig' a handful of times. Seems impossible doesn't it because the book is riddled with the words? If you look back now you'll see that I actually always said 'guinea *pigs*', plural. This is because I was sneakily trying to get into your brain and make you always think about lots of guinea pigs, not just one. Sadly, for thousands and thousands of guinea pigs humans have got it wrong for a very long time. In the past, and, I'm afraid to say, still today, guinea pigs have been and still are kept on their own. You need to immediately wipe this from your mind because the one thing you need to remember from this chapter is this;

Guinea pigs should NEVER be kept on their own.

Now there might be occasional times they have to be alone for a short while like if one of them is poorly but in general for everyday life they should have at least one guinea pig friend, if not more.

Let's do what we should always do and think back to our wild guinea pigs. They live in close groups of very good friends and family. They are prey animals and find safety in numbers. This means they feel safest when there are other guinea pigs around. Think back to how they communicate and work together. If there is more than one of them they have extra eyes and ears to look out for predators. If they know someone else is on watch they can relax a little and graze and feel secure. This means they can get plenty to eat, keep their teeth and intestines healthy and stay safe all at the same time.

Not only are they prey animals, needing numbers to feel safe, they actually really like other guinea pigs. They are sociable animals. They like to play together which for pet guinea pigs means they will stay fitter and slimmer. They can run and chase around, especially in that brilliant enclosure you are going to build them! Life should be fun for them.

It's fun to explore with friends.

THE NEED TO BE WITH OR WITHOUT OTHER ANIMALS.

Staying close means staying warm.

Guinea pigs love to snuggle, just the same as us humans. It not only makes them feel safe and happy but especially in cold weather, it keeps them warm. Guinea pigs are small animals and small animals lose heat more quickly than big animals. This is because they have a big body surface compared to their size. By snuggling together they can share warmth and slow down the loss of heat from their little bodies.

Everyone has places that are hard to reach!

Guinea pigs also love to groom each other. They can do some of it for themselves but like all of us they have places that are difficult to reach or see like their face, eyes and ears.

You can imagine that if you only have your tongue and your paws to wash with, having a friend to help is always going to make life easier. Grooming each other helps keep their fur in tiptop condition but is also an important part of guinea pig life. It helps them form relationships, bond with each other and keep the group tightly knitted together. If you do get some pet guinea pigs if you have time and patience they will sometimes learn to love you grooming them, just the same as their friends.

You might find it hard to believe but us humans are quite similar to guinea pigs in lots of ways. Deep down inside we are still prey animals. We have lots of ways and lots of knowledge these days to help us avoid being eaten but there are still plenty of animals that could make a meal of us if we got too close. We still feel scared of things like the dark or spiders and even when we try to tell ourselves we don't need to be afraid we still are sometimes. This is because our bodies are still ready to avoid danger so we still get that racing heart and sweaty feeling when we feel under threat. You might remember when we talked about how you would feel if you had to walk past the school bully. Would you feel confident to do it on your own or would you feel safer if you were in a crowd of friends?

Young guinea pigs stick close together like you and your friends.

And we are social creatures. Ok, some of us don't seem very friendly, but on the whole humans like to be near other humans. You can have fun on your own but the best laughs and happiest times tend to be with other people. We like to share experiences, swap stories and news and maybe most importantly play together. When we are sad, frightened or poorly we usually need other people even more. When everything seems bad a warm hug from someone you love is usually the best medicine.

So although we said we shouldn't assume animals' needs are *exactly* the same as ours we can still empathise with them. This means we can imagine how they might feel in some situations because we know how we would feel. I'm sure you can imagine how you'd feel if you spent your whole life alone. You could definitely survive but you would probably at times be frightened, grumpy, sad, bored or frustrated and feel like there was something missing. You would probably go a little bit mad to be honest.

So imagine yourself, living alone in your empty bedroom and to be kind someone decided to put a donkey in your bedroom to keep you company. Bear with me, I am going somewhere with this! You can't understand what a donkey 'says' and a donkey can't understand your ramblings either. If you got too close or tried to cuddle him he might bite you or kick you and really hurt you. You might spend all your time squeezed up into a corner just to try and stay out of his way. This is what it's like for guinea pigs which are kept with rabbits for company.

Over the years lots of people with all the best intentions have kept guinea pigs and rabbits together. They are totally different animals! They don't communicate in the same way, they have different needs when it comes to food and they don't live together in the wild. They can both hurt each other with bites but rabbits are like the donkey in your bedroom. They are much bigger, much stronger and can badly injure and even kill guinea pigs. Please don't keep them together. If you like rabbits find out all about their needs and learn how to keep them happy and healthy with other rabbits, not guinea pigs. In the meantime let's concentrate on the piggies!

Now you're really empathising with those lonely guinea pigs which are kept on their own, imagine how happy they would feel if they had a proper guinea pig friend or two.

THE NEED TO BE WITH OR WITHOUT OTHER ANIMALS.

If you or one of your friends already has a lonely guinea pig don't worry, all is not lost. You can nearly always introduce another guinea pig and if you do it the right way they will usually become firm friends very quickly.

Lots of animals that live in groups have what's called a pecking order. This means that they all know who is the boss, who is next most important and so on all the way to the bottom of the heap. The term pecking order comes from chickens and the way they organise themselves. The top chicken gets to peck at any food first and then the next in line and so on. A bit like an orderly queue at a bus stop! You don't need to feel sorry for the animals who aren't at the top; lots of animals don't mind where they are in the pecking order as long as they know their place. It's an important way that social animals get along and don't end up fighting all the time. Humans are just the same in some situations. At your school you'll have a head teacher and everyone else knows they are in charge. This stops all your other teachers arguing about who's going to make the big decisions.

Guinea pigs are just the same. In any group there will be pigs which are dominant and higher up the pecking order and ones which are what's called subordinate and lower down. When guinea pigs first meet they size each other up and sometimes have a little rough and tumble to figure out which one is boss. Usually once they've decided who's who they will live very happily together.

© C and C cages

Using a split cage helps introduce new guinea pig friends.

Lots of animal adoption and rehoming centres have guinea pigs looking for homes just the same as cats and dogs. By adopting a guinea pig you or your friend will be doing a double good deed; giving two guinea pigs a happy life with a friend and donating some money to a worthy cause at the same time. Talk to your vet about the best way to introduce them.

In general it's best to have a pair or a group of females or a pair of males. You can keep groups of females with one male but he will have to be neutered. This is an operation to stop him being able to make babies. You can't add any more males because they will try and fight over the ladies. We'll talk more about neutering guinea pigs in chapter 7. If you are planning a group you will need plenty of space so everyone can have some peace and quiet and get away from any of the others who might be bugging them.

You might be thinking that I keep saying I'm going to talk about environmental enrichment then forgetting. I haven't forgotten at all. Keeping guinea pigs in pairs or more is the best way to enrich their environment there is! They can play, chase, watch out for each other, keep warm and groom. What we're actually saying is that they can suddenly do loads of natural behaviours which they not only enjoy but that they feel the *need* to do. And this leads us on to the rest of enrichment and what it's actually all about. It's about need number 4; the need to behave naturally. And I'm sure now you can understand why an animal's social needs are so entwined with behaviour. If you're a social creature you want to do fun things with your friends!

© Liz Yates

Having friends means lots of mischievous fun!

THE NEED TO EXPRESS NORMAL BEHAVIOUR.

Have you ever had an itch in a place you couldn't reach? Right in between your shoulder blades for example. You bend your arm right the way up your back but the tip of your thumb stops about a centimetre short of the itchy spot. Ooooohh, it drives you mad doesn't it? You try and ignore it but the more you try the more you keep thinking about it until you can't think about anything else. Eventually your mum finds you crazily scraping yourself up and down the door frame or discovers you have roped her best hairbrush to a wooden spoon and are frantically gouging it up and down your back with a weird look on your face like a cross between sheer panic and total heaven.

This is what it's like for animals who are not allowed to do the things they love or feel the need to do. It's the itch they can never scratch. All animals are born with some behaviours that are what's called 'innate'. This means they are born needing to do something even if they don't know why. Other behaviours are learnt as they grow. For example, an innate behaviour for children appears to be constantly picking your nose, whereas a learnt one is getting a tissue and actually wiping it!

Innate behaviours help animals get a head start because they can do things without needing to be shown. One of the strongest and earliest innate behaviours you see is when animals suckle their mother's milk. Within minutes of being born, calves, lambs, kittens, puppies and human babies all start looking for their first warm drink of milk. They don't think about why and they don't need to but it gives them a great start because they get a full tummy and lots of goodness straight away.

The important thing to remember is that even if we keep an animal in a way that means it doesn't *need* to do something any more it will still feel the urge to do it. It will still be the itch they can't scratch. For instance you might absolutely know that your guinea pigs will always be totally safe from predators but they will still want and need to hide away because for all they know, especially at the start, *you* might even be a predator. If they can't hide they'll be really frightened.

Our pets should be free to have as much fun and be as happy as possible as well as not feeling frightened. Think back to all the things we've mentioned that guinea pigs enjoy. Exploring, grooming, running, popcorning, hiding, stretching out, grazing, relaxing, cuddling and the list goes on. So now let's look at all the ways we can make it happen for them. Or in other words, all the ways we can enrich their environment. See, I haven't forgotten!

You've hopefully learnt that a small hutch or cage is not going to do much for them and with a big hutch and an attached large run or in your indoor palace you've created they can run, stretch up, stretch out and explore.

Having friends means lots of mischievous fun!

We know after the last chapter that they need to have a friend or two and that's definitely going to tick some things off our list. They can groom and cuddle and play.

© C and C cages
A big cage is brilliant but you need to add fun things.

But even the biggest run is still going to be pretty small compared to what they would cover in the wild and it will be pretty samey every day so you need to make it interesting and you need to change it around once in a while to keep it interesting.

THE NEED TO EXPRESS NORMAL BEHAVIOUR.

Being outside lets your guinea pigs explore and graze naturally.

© RWAF

A hanging basket makes a great hay net...

You'll be giving them some vegetables and other leafy plants every day too. It's also essential to have hay available for them all the time. This might be in their hutch but you can get little hay racks for the run too so they have plenty of choice. The run and their environment is your chance to be really creative. Your mum or dad might have an old hanging basket. You could dangle it from the roof of the run to use as a hay rack and keep the hay nice and dry. Remember to make sure it's low enough for them to easily reach though.

You can let them find safe, tasty herbs and plants to eat.

© Cagetopia™

...or indoors you could have something completely different!

Hopefully if they're outdoors your run will be on some grass so they can graze and maybe even forage around for some other plants as well as grass.

Don't just give them their veg or pellets in a bowl. Have a look in the pet shop or be inventive at home. Hide their food in cardboard tunnels or scatter it among some grass or hay so they can explore and enjoy hunting around to get their food.

You can buy fancy hides...

We've said that guinea pigs sometimes borrow other animals' burrows or tunnel through long grass and that's where they feel safe so make them some tunnels. Cardboard tubes or boxes with holes are an easy way to give them places to hide and explore. You can buy tunnel systems from pet shops if you have enough money. You can even make tunnels leading from the hutch to the run or from the big run to another smaller run somewhere else.

...or you can use a cardboard box or an old hollow log!

41

Chapter 6

THE NEED TO EXPRESS NORMAL BEHAVIOUR.

Challenge yourself to see how inventive you can be. If you're feeling extra inventive you could even ask your mum or dad if you could plant some meadow grass like Timothy grass in a patch of the garden where the run might be. This way you would be creating an exciting natural habitat for them to hide in, explore and nibble.

The great thing about environmental enrichment is that you can let your imagination go wild. There is nothing better in the world than seeing a happy pet and you'll soon see when you've made them happy.

Guinea pigs in the wild will climb onto logs to have a look around.

As well as hiding places guinea pigs also like lookout posts or platforms. You can put things like a log in the run so they can climb on and off. If your guinea pigs had a small hutch when you got them you could stand that in the run as a place to explore or sit on. You'll need to make a secure ramp up to it for them to climb. All this clambering up and down is good exercise and will help to keep them slim but also keep their bones strong. When they are on top of the platform they can have a good look round or just relax, it's their choice! You could put a hide box up there too. Just make sure all the wood you use has no chemicals on it because they'll get chewed for sure.

Pet shops sell lots of toys for guinea pigs so go for it. Don't overwhelm them though, it's important to keep things interesting. You know yourself how soon a new toy can lose its appeal and how exciting it is if you're lucky enough to get a new present so keep that in mind. Put a couple of toys in the run but change them every few days. You can always put the old ones back in again the next week. They'll still be interesting after a break.

© Cagetopia™

Keep some toys and hides out of the cage so you can rotate them for interest.

You can try all sorts, as long as you're putting things in that are safe. Why not give them a sturdy ball to nudge about? You can buy balls to put their pellets in with holes to let the food drop out as they nudge it around. This is way more fun than just giving them their rations in a boring dish.

Guinea pigs in the wild sometimes chew bark from trees as well as grazing and you can get lots of different chews for your guinea pigs in all sorts of shapes and sizes. You don't need to spend a fortune. You could find out what the pet shop sells and then see if you can do a homemade version. As we said, you might have some logs at home your mum or dad could chop up for you. Just make sure you know what wood you have so you can find out if it's safe for them. One of the behaviours that most kids love to do is making things. Why not combine *your* needs for fun with your guinea pigs' needs and see how spectacular you can be? You can always send your pictures in to thepetsite.co.uk to compare with the other creative pet detectives out there.

...or you can use a cardboard box or an old hollow log!

Beautiful big cages still need cleaning out and your pigs will still need some messy floor time!

These behavioural needs are very important for the happiness of your guinea pigs and you might need to consider them even more if you're thinking about keeping your guinea pigs indoors. They're still going to need lookouts, hay, places to explore, hiding places, friends and space to run and play. Guinea pigs are notoriously messy creatures, they get in their food bowls, they're not easy to litter train like rabbits and you and your family need to think carefully about where you want to keep them. Some people devote a whole room to them but you need to be sure you can cope with the mess. Even if they're in a very large cage they'll still need floor time and all this could be quite a mission when it comes to cleaning up!

Whenever you think about your pet's happiness I think it's good to think about yours. Always remember that surviving is not enough, being happy is just as important. Always try and think about how you would feel if you couldn't do the things you really enjoy or see the people you like and love. It's not ok to deprive an animal of something it needs just because we don't like it or it's inconvenient for us. Remember we said that you should never ask yourself what sort of pet you want, only what sort of pet you can keep truly happy and healthy. Blimey, I went all serious again then didn't I? Well, it's good to be serious sometimes because as we said, looking after animals is a serious business! So now you fabulous fact finders know EVERYTHING there is to know about wild guinea pigs and how to keep pet guinea pigs *happy*, we better get down to that other very important bit where we find out how to keep them *healthy* too!

THE NEED TO BE PROTECTED FROM PAIN, INJURY AND DISEASE.

Every person and every animal gets poorly or hurt from time to time. That's just a simple fact of being alive. I always tell my daughters that their bumped shins and skinned knees are a good sign they've been having plenty of fun. We already talked about what amazing machines bodies are and one of their most amazing abilities is how they can heal and recover from injuries and disease. But you'll all know already that there are lots of illnesses and injuries that bodies can't cope with and that bodies need extra help with. It's not just about getting help for your pets when they are poorly or hurt, it's very important to find out all the ways you can stop them from getting ill in the first place.

We said before that guinea pigs might not like being handled much and carried about but it is also important to make sure your guinea pigs are used to being handled for health reasons. You will need to check them over regularly to make sure they are healthy and they will need to go to the vet sometimes. If they are used to humans and being carefully picked up and examined they will be less stressed and less likely to struggle and injure you or themselves.

Remember guinea pigs are prey animals so if they are picked up from above they feel like they've been caught and will be more likely to try to get away. Always approach quietly and carefully from the side. Slide one hand under their chest and use the other to make sure their bottom is supported. Never let them dangle when you pick them up. It's a good idea to go to your vet as soon as possible when you get your guinea pigs. They can have a good check over and you can watch and learn how to handle them best. If you are unsure always get a grown-up to help you.

Guinea pigs in general are pretty healthy, robust little creatures when cared for properly. For example they don't need vaccinations like people and many animals do against serious infectious diseases. But you may have guessed from some of the things we've learned so far that there are still certain things they need or problems they could be prone to when kept as pets.

Let's look at prevention first and then we can have a look at signs to watch out for that might mean your guinea pigs are under the weather.

Scurvy

As we mentioned when we were talking about food, guinea pigs, like humans and some other animals, can't make their own vitamin C. This vitamin is really important for lots of things from skin health to a strong immune system to fight off disease. If your guinea pigs don't get enough vitamin C in a good, balanced diet they get a disease called scurvy. This is a very nasty disease, is very painful and can easily kill your guinea pigs if it's missed or not treated. Signs include skin problems, bad gums, bleeding, weakness and eventually death.

Luckily, scurvy is very easy to prevent by following all the advice in chapter 3 about vegetables and plants rich in vitamin C and feeding the right sorts of pellets. Just bear it in mind and you can make sure your guinea pigs don't end up like those sailors of old!

Mange, mites and lice

Pretty much every animal on the planet, including us humans (especially children!) gets various kinds of parasites, and guinea pigs are no different. Parasites are animals or plants that live on or in another animal or plant. They include things like worms, lice, mites and fleas. Guinea pigs occasionally get lice which cause hair loss and itching but the biggest problem we see is with mites.

When guinea pigs get mites it's also called mange. These mites cause unbearable itchiness. Your guinea pigs can get so miserable with all the itching and scratching that they can make themselves bleed, get covered in scabs and sores and lose masses of fur. Most guinea pigs will come into contact with the odd mite on bedding or in the environment and most healthy, strong pigs will get rid of the creatures quite easily without you ever knowing. Very young, very old or weak, poorly animals won't manage to get rid of them. The mites soon multiply and cause lots of problems. If you notice bald patches or itching you should get your pigs to the vet straight away. Not only might they have mites but it could be a sign of other problems like a lack of vitamin C.

These days it's pretty easy to get rid of these parasites but you must ALWAYS talk to your vet about what to use. Some of the medicines and chemicals we use on dogs and cats can easily kill small animals like guinea pigs so be very careful. Mites and lice are usually passed onto the animals on infested bedding or on things which have been in contact with an infected guinea pig. Always use good quality, fresh bedding and wash your hands after touching other people's guinea pigs and this will help prevent them getting the parasites in the first place.

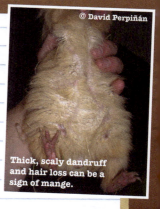

Thick, scaly dandruff and hair loss can be a sign of mange.

Tooth problems, fat guinea pigs and fly strike

Now these sound like very different problems don't they? Well, they are but they also have one huge thing in common so I think we should look at them all together. If you think back to some of the things we've said in chapter 3 you might have an idea what it is. That's right. DIET again! So, if you've taken on board all of chapter 3 and when we talked about scurvy, I won't need to say too much because you are already ahead of the game.

Tooth problems used to be a huge issue for pet guinea pigs because we didn't understand how important grinding and chewing were along with the right diet. And obviously today if we get their diet wrong, tooth problems can still cause pain, abscesses and even death. We said before that guinea pigs' teeth never stop growing because they have evolved to eat grass and tough plants which need lots of chewing. If you feed things like muesli or lots of soft, sugary fruit and not enough long fibre like hay and grass your guinea pigs' teeth will not get worn down enough. This means they get too long and will start to curl in all sorts of directions in the guinea pig's mouth. They get very sharp and grow into all the soft, tender bits of the mouth like the tongue, lips and cheeks. If you've ever bitten your tongue or cheek by accident you'll know how sore this is so imagine if you had that pain all the time.

Often the bad diet that lets the teeth get too long also doesn't have all the right vitamins and minerals and this can make weak bones and tooth sockets. The long teeth start to get loose and infection can get into the pockets the teeth sit in causing big, painful abscesses full of pus in the jaw and gums. Ouch! The guinea pigs won't be able to eat and will quickly get weak, thin and really poorly. Once the teeth get this bad it can be almost impossible to make them right again and many guinea pigs like this end up being put to sleep so it's very important to stop it happening in the first place. You won't be able to see your guinea pigs' back teeth so if you have any worries get your vet to check them for you.

Thinking back you'll remember we said that animals being too fat is very bad for them. Being too fat or obese puts extra strain on joints, bones and the heart and shortens life. It can cause quite a few diseases in various animals and in guinea pigs especially it causes some very big problems. Now you probably felt

© Emma Keeble

Very long incisor teeth make eating impossible.

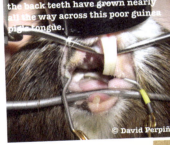

Only the right tools let us see how the back teeth have grown nearly all the way across this poor guinea pig's tongue.

© David Perpiñá

a bit sick when you thought about eating your own poo all the way back in chapter 2 but for guinea pigs it is essential. As we said they have to digest their food twice to get all the goodness out of it. To do this they eat one type of soft poo straight from their bottom then the next time it comes out it is the hard, shiny droppings that we are used to seeing. If a guinea pig is too fat it can't even reach its bottom in the first place. This means two things; the pig misses out on some goodness because the poo doesn't get eaten and the soft, sticky poo stays round the bottom and gets stuck in the fur and on the fat skin

© Emma Keeble

A horribly fat pet guinea pig...

© Emma Keeble

and also makes the bedding and hutch a pooey mess.

I'm sure you can imagine that being covered in your own poo is not very nice for any animals but it can also cause something far more serious for guinea pigs and that is something called fly strike. Some flies love to lay their eggs in poo as part of their life cycle. The eggs hatch out into maggots and the maggots are very hungry. Sadly for pooey guinea pigs the thing the maggots are hungry for is flesh. The maggots crawl through the poo onto the skin and they start to literally eat the guinea pigs alive. I don't need to tell you how horrible this would be for them.

Now, you might think that fly strike would be totally obvious and you'd notice straight away but you'd be wrong because there is another fact about some prey animals that we haven't mentioned yet; they don't show pain like we do. Now if you or I, or a predator like a dog or cat for instance, had a big cut or a broken leg or we were being eaten alive by maggots we would be howling, crying, limping and generally carrying on as much as we could to get sympathy and help. Not guinea pigs. Cuts and poorly legs and injuries in general make prey animals much more likely to get caught and eaten because they are not fully fit to get away. Because of this lots of prey animals will not cry out or limp because they are so much more likely to attract a predator. Your pet guinea pigs still have this innate behaviour even though they have you to look after them. Very often one of the signs of the guinea pigs who are the most ill or the most in pain is just that they are very quiet and don't move around much.

Sadly, lots of people don't look at their guinea pigs often enough to notice these things and by the time the fly strike is discovered it can be absolutely horrific. So how can we prevent it?

DIET! The right diet and exercise will keep your guinea pigs healthy and slim so they shouldn't get covered in poo. You'll also need to check the hutch or cage every day to make sure there is no soiled bedding attracting flies. Insect screens and fly papers can also help.

Talk to your vet as well as they may have repellents which are safe to put round your guinea pigs' bottoms to be extra safe. We all know how annoying flies are and how easily they get inside the house so remember that indoor guinea pigs are just as at risk as those kept outdoors.

The *most* important thing to do when it comes to fly strike and keeping guinea pigs in general is to make sure you look at them! This might sound simple but when it's a bit cold or you've got a friend over after school or your favourite TV programme is on it can get easily forgotten. You should look at your guinea pigs' whole bodies every day and when the flies are about you should look at them twice a day. And this means carefully handling them and actually checking there are no poo, eggs or maggots anywhere in sight.

...compared with a beautifully slim wild one.

Neutering

Neutering is when your pet has an operation to make sure he or she can't have any babies. Vets recommend that many pets like dogs, cats and rabbits are neutered because it helps reduce the number of unwanted or neglected pets. For lots of animals it can also stop them getting certain diseases like cancer and can help keep them healthier.

Guinea pigs are a bit more complicated and if you keep pairs of the same sex you don't need to have them neutered unless there is a medical reason. For instance, female guinea pigs are quite prone to cysts on their ovaries, where they make their eggs. These cysts can make them look really fat but also make hormones which can make them go bald down their sides and on their tummies. These are the most common reason for neutering female guinea pigs.

If you plan to have a group of sows with a boar you need to have the boar neutered or you'll soon be over-run with babies and that wouldn't be the responsible thing to do! Talk to your vet about when to have the male guinea pig neutered and what you need to do to help him get well soon after his trip to the surgery.

© David Perpiñán

Two guinea pigs with swollen tummies and bald sides from ovarian cysts.

© David Perpiñán

Bumblefoot

This might sound like a character from Harry Potter but it's actually a horrible, painful disease that guinea pigs can easily get if their hutch, cage or run is not right. The fancy, sciency name for it is pododermatitis but we'll stick to bumblefoot because it's easier to say!

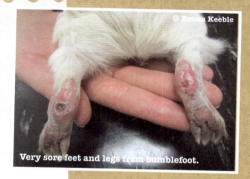
© Emma Keeble
Very sore feet and legs from bumblefoot.

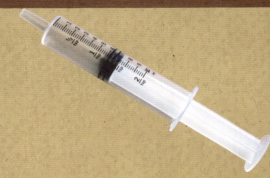

Bumblefoot is what happens when guinea pigs are kept on hard floors or wire-bottomed cages. They have sensitive little feet and in the wild live on soft, grassy plains and sandy soils. When they have wire to walk on or not enough bedding their feet get little cuts and grazes. These get infected and the bacteria which invade the cuts make painful abscesses and sore feet. These will make your guinea pigs lame, be very miserable and can be difficult to treat. As always, prevention is better than cure. Being the brilliant detectives you are, I'm sure your guinea pigs will have palaces to live in and beautifully looked after feet but now you know another reason why fact finding is so important.

Are your guinea pigs healthy?

The things we've mentioned so far are the big things to be aware of when it comes to having pet guinea pigs but there are all sorts of diseases, conditions and injuries that can happen. If you want to learn about every single one then you should do your homework, work hard and become a vet because I haven't got room for all of it here! The best way to keep your pets healthy in general is to be observant and know what's normal so you can quickly spot when things are wrong. As we said, guinea pigs can be very brave when it comes to not showing illness so it's up to you to spot the little changes in the look or behaviour of your guinea pigs so you can get on top of problems quickly. Smaller animals like guinea pigs can get weak and ill very quickly so if you are ever worried, take them to the vet. Your vet won't think you're silly if there's nothing wrong. It's always better to be safe than sorry.

THE NEED TO BE PROTECTED FROM PAIN, INJURY AND DISEASE.

Things to watch for in your guinea pigs themselves;

🐾 Bright eyes. Guinea pigs are quite prone to scratches on the surface of their eyes, especially from straw and hay.

© Emma Keeble

Scratches on the surface of the eye can turn into bluish ulcers like this.

Watch out for runny eyes or discharge, swelling round the eyelids or redness. These could be signs of infections or scratches but it can also be a because of tooth root problems as well.

🐾 Clean nose. No snot or mucus coming from either side, no lumps or bumps.

🐾 Shiny, clean fur. Your guinea pigs will groom themselves and each other but depending on the type of guinea pigs you have you might need to groom them too, especially when they are moulting. Grooming can help you make friends with your guinea pigs and is a good way to check them over. In general, check the fur has no mats or things stuck in it. If you see bald patches, dandruff or scabs they could have mites or lice and need to go to your vet straight away. Short-haired guinea pigs are much easier to keep tangle free and have a much more natural coat. Long-haired guinea pigs are really best avoided. Look out for wet fur under the chin. This could be a sign of drooling and dribbling and tooth problems.

🐾 Comfortable, clean ears. If your guinea pigs' ears seem dirty or itchy or you see them keep shaking their heads they could have ear mites or an ear infection. This sometimes also gives them a head tilt. Time for a trip to the vet.

🐾 Body Condition Score or BCS. It's really good to understand body condition. It's a way of talking about how fat or thin your animals are. Most people have a scale of 1-5 where 1 is dangerously thin, 3 is normal and 5 is dangerously obese. Lots of people misjudge BCS so ask your vet how you can tell what the scores look and feel like on your guinea pigs. Keeping your guinea pigs in the right body condition is essential for good health.

🐾 Make sure your guinea pigs don't have any sore patches anywhere. You need to check all over and on their joints and feet.

- Make sure their nails are not overgrown. Depending on how much exercise your guinea pigs do and the places they live they might occasionally need their nails cut. Your vet or vet nurse will be happy to tell you if they need doing.

- Check for poo round the bottom and for fly eggs or maggots. Every day and twice daily in the summer.

- Short, even teeth. As we said, you'll need your vet to check the back teeth but if you gently lift your guinea pigs' lips at the front you'll be able to see their front teeth. These should be straight, short and symmetrical.

- Normal breathing. As we said, guinea pigs don't like extremes of temperature, draughts or damp. They can easily get chest infections so try to get used to what normal breathing is like. If they are breathing fast or seem to be putting a lot of effort into it they should go to a vet.

- Look out for odd behaviour. This could be anything from being 'a bit quiet' to hunched, not eating, not moving around as normal, stiff, floppy, teeth grinding, sneezing. Basically anything out of the ordinary. If you see any weird or unusual behaviour get your guinea pigs to the vet as soon as you can.

Things to watch for in your guinea pigs' surroundings;

- Normal faeces (poo) and urine (wee). Guinea pigs can get bladder stones especially if they're fed the wrong things. If you see blood in the wee or if you think your pigs are having trouble getting their wee out you need to go straight to a vet. If you see the soft sticky faeces a lot of the time then it could be a sign of trouble. Diarrhoea is a definite sign that all is not well. Once again, you'll soon get used to what's normal for your guinea pigs. If you don't look you don't know!

- Dropped or half chewed food. If you find clumps of half chewed food it could be a sign that one or more of your guinea pigs has tooth problems.

Don't panic about all these things; the more you get to know your guinea pigs the sooner and more easily you'll spot the odd things. The better an owner you are, the healthier your guinea pigs will be and hopefully the fewer trips to the vet you'll need. Remember that you can't get guinea pigs and just forget about them. You need to be around them at least once a day, check them over and make sure they are safe, protected and well. If in doubt, ask your vet.

Now you have all the facts about wild guinea pigs and you know how to keep your pet guinea pigs happy as well as healthy. So it must be time for even more fact-finding, some virtual reality and some good old maths. Basically it's time to actually answer that crucial question;

Are guinea pigs the right pet for me and my family?

ARE GUINEA PIGS THE RIGHT PET FOR ME AND MY FAMILY?

In this chapter we're going to crunch some numbers and you're going to have to start investigating facts from some other places besides this book. We're also going to embark on a virtual month of being a guinea pig owner. You might feel silly but it's a brilliant way of checking if you actually do have what it takes to be a dedicated owner of guinea pigs. You can do it all by yourself or you can involve the whole family in the decisions, care and sums.

If you find yourself, towards the end of the virtual month, getting a bit bored with pretending to check over, feed, handle and groom a teddy once or twice a day remember this; well cared for pet guinea pigs usually live about five years but can live up to eight years, so you need to get used to it!

Week One — How Much??!

We'll spend the first week finding out some costs to ease you into it gently. Some of these costs are definitely a one off like neutering. Things like buying the hutch or cage and run might seem like that too but bear in mind that over five years some things might wear out and need replacing so a bit of reserve is always needed. Things like toys are good to rotate or renew so try to get an idea of the cost of say three average toys and allow that amount every month.

Now is also the time to consider right from the outset how much room you have. If you don't have the space for the big hutch or shed and run or you've decided the house is not the right place for guinea pigs then you might not need to go much further and can avoid the painful maths! So, assuming you have the room here's a place to start filling in those numbers. The boxes which are coloured in green are either one off costs or costs which will only need to be rarely repeated. This will help you and your family get an idea of how much your initial outlay is likely to be compared to ongoing costs. Don't forget though that virtually everything will need to be paid for at the start so add everything together for your startup costs!

Things to find out from the pet shop/adoption centre or the internet

Item	Cost £
The piggies! Bear in mind that adoption centre costs may include neutering. Remember to multiply the cost for the number of guinea pigs you are planning to have.	
Hutch, cage or shed. Remember you need a minimum size of 1.2m x 0.7m x 0.5m for two guinea pigs. More pigs will need more!	
Run or materials to build one. Minimum size of 2m x 2m.	
Tunnels if you're planning to have tunnels linking smaller exercise areas.	
Bedding. Try to find out roughly how long a bag will last so you can work out monthly costs for your mum and dad.	
Good quality hay. Try to find out roughly how long a bag will last so you can work out monthly costs for your mum and dad.	
Pellets. Try to find out roughly how long a bag will last so you can work out monthly costs for your mum and dad.	
Veg. You'll need to ask your parents this one. They'll need to buy extra veg to make sure your guinea pigs get a good variety.	
Food bowls or scatter balls.	
Water bowls and bottles.	
Hay nets or hanging baskets.	
Toys and chews. Find out how often chews will need replacing and get an idea how much toys cost to allow for occasional replacements.	
Brushes or gloves for grooming.	
Fly screens and papers for the summer.	
Total	

ARE GUINEA PIGS THE RIGHT PET FOR ME AND MY FAMILY?

Things to find out from your vet

Procedure	Cost £
Neutering. This is only needed if you are planning to keep males and females together. It's worth finding out how much it costs anyway just in case they need to be neutered later in life.	
Fly repellent (if available).	
Nail trim. Find out how often they feel it usually needs doing.	
Normal consultation. Many people think guinea pigs are cheaper to have examined by a vet when they are poorly but most charge the same as for a dog or cat so it's worth finding out what that cost is.	
Total from this and the last page added together	

These numbers may be a bit mindbogglingly big when you look at them but that's why I wanted you to do it. There is no such thing as a cheap pet. Obviously you will have worked out that once you're all set up your monthly costs may be much more manageable but don't forget about vets' fees and unexpected problems. Guinea pigs are definitely cheaper than some pets but they will still cost about £2000 or sometimes more over their lifetime and remember that you need to have more than one!

Week Two — Handle with Care

This week you are going to spend time and energy devoted to your new (pretend!) guinea pigs and getting to know them. It's important to get your guinea pigs used to being handled right from a young age. As we said in the last chapter this will help them feel safe and secure with you and not feel threatened. If they are happy being handled gently they will be much less likely to scratch or bite you and also less likely to hurt themselves thrashing to get away from you. It will also make them feel less stressed when they need to go to the vet and be handled by strangers. This week you will need to spend about half an hour, morning and evening, getting to know your guinea pigs (teddies!). Practice how you would approach and pick them up. Remember to stay quiet and move gently and calmly. Look online and see if you can find videos of how to handle guinea pigs. You should be able to groom them, hold them safely and learn how to gently examine them to make sure they are well.

Most of the time should be used to just stroke and groom them to help with bonding and to start with you might find it best just to spend some time quietly near your guinea pigs so that they get used to your smell and the look of you. Offering a tasty piece of fresh veg out of their ration when you handle them will help your guinea pigs see you as a real goodie rather than a possible predator! Try to look out for signs of when your guinea pigs have had enough. All animals vary and your guinea pigs might not be interested in cuddles and grooming from you. If they are like this remember to respect their needs and be happy just to watch them having fun together.

As well as the nice contact time, once or twice a day depending on the time of year you will also need to examine them for all the things we said to look out for in chapter 7. You will need to briefly look at their bottoms and their underneath for poo or sores but try not to take too long to do this because guinea pigs don't feel safe on their backs. You want the majority of the time they are with you to be a pleasant experience for both of you! You'll almost certainly find it easier to get a grown up to help you look underneath. If one person holds the guinea pig they can gently tip it upwards, always supporting its bottom, while you have a careful look round the back end. When you've got your real guinea pigs, if you decide to go ahead, this will be the time when you'll really start to get to know how your guinea pigs feel and how they behave. Once they are used to you and being handled you can start to let them have their floor time. You need to be sure you can safely get them back to their cage without frightening them or chasing them.

By handling them every day you'll soon spot when things are not right and if they feel skinnier or fatter than they should. You'll also start to get used to the language they speak and will start to understand what all their wonderful sounds mean. A chirpy greeting from your pigs is a wonderful thing to hear and something to really look forward to.

ARE GUINEA PIGS THE RIGHT PET FOR ME AND MY FAMILY?

Here is a table to fill in for this week. Once you are in the swing of things you'll find that most of the body check becomes part of your normal handling time and you add the bottom check as an extra. Oh yes, and don't forget to wash your hands afterwards!

Job/Day	Monday	Tuesday	Wednesday	Thursday	Friday	Saturday	Sunday
Time nearby, stroking, grooming AM	✓						
Time nearby, stroking, grooming PM	✓						
Full body check AM or PM	✓						
Bottom check (should be done twice daily in fly season)	✓						
Front teeth and claw check (once a week)	✗	x	x	x	x	x	

Week Three — Fed, Watered and Neat as a Pin!

This week you'll be doing the dirty work! As well as feeding and checking the water is fresh and clean you'll be learning about cleaning up. It's a rare person who really enjoys cleaning anything so you can be forgiven for not looking forward to this but it is a huge part of pet keeping. There is no getting away from the fact that some of what goes in has to come out and it is up to you to clear it up! Handling poo and sometimes wee can make you poorly so you need to make sure you know all about hygiene. Always wear gloves to clean out your hutch or cage and the run and always wash your hands afterwards. Look back at chapter 3 if you need to remind yourself about how much of which foods to give if you can't remember.

Of course you still don't have any guinea pigs so this week is about setting aside the time you need as if you had to do these jobs. Why not get your mum or dad to give you a boring job to do that would take about the same amount of time. Clean the bathroom, including the loo, empty all the bins or do the ironing. You'll get an idea of the more boring side of being a pet owner and you'll get massive brownie points at the same time. Also remember that if your guinea pigs will be kept outside, lots of these jobs will need to be done in the semi dark and cold. You can't be a fairweather pet owner!

Checklist for this week

Job/Day	Monday	Tuesday	Wednesday	Thursday	Friday	Saturday	Sunday
Check/give food AM							
Check/give food PM							
Give fresh water and clean bowls AM							
Check/freshen water and clean bowls if necessary PM							
Remove soiled bedding once daily and top up bedding if need be							
Wash food bowls and water bottles once daily (at least)							
Clean out whole hutch and replace bedding (once a week)	x	x	x	x	x	x	
Check toys, chews and enrichment and replace if necessary (once a week)	x	x	x	x	x	x	

This is also the time to look online and find out about which plants, veg and fruits are safe and which are poisonous for guinea pigs. Look at what's in your garden and identify the plants if you're going to let your guinea pigs roam or feed them plants from your garden. Here is a place to make your lists.

Safe	Poisonous
Apples, cucumber,	Meat,

Week Four — EVERYTHING!!

And now for the grand finale. This week you will need to find an hour or two every day in your hectic schedule to devote to your new pets. Fill in the rather large table below and add in your ongoing costs at the bottom. Most of all try to enjoy it because if you do get some guinea pigs you're going to be doing this for years, not weeks, and possibly even until you leave home!

Job/Day	Monday	Tuesday	Wednesday	Thursday	Friday	Saturday	Sunday
Time nearby, stroking, grooming AM							
Time nearby, stroking, grooming PM							
Full body check AM or PM							
Bottom check (should be done twice daily in fly season)							
Front teeth and claw check (once a week)							
Check/give food AM							
Check/give food PM							
Give fresh water AM							
Check/freshen water PM							
Remove soiled bedding/empty litter tray once daily and top up bedding							
Wash bowls once daily (at least)							
Clean out whole hutch and replace bedding (once a week)							
Check toys, chews and enrichment and replace if necessary (once a week)							
Costs £							

Time for the Family Debate

Over the last few weeks and having read the rest of the book you should now have some idea of what keeping guinea pigs is actually about. If you're like most people you'll probably be quite shocked. It's very rare for people to realise just how much time and money is needed to look after pets well. Anyone can look after pets badly but I hope that now you will most definitely not be one of them!

You've probably been talking to your family about things as you've gone along but if not now is the time to do that. You can call a meeting and present your facts, like all the best detectives do. Because now you really do have everything you need to answer that question. And to answer it honestly. Things you might want to talk about at your family meeting:

- If you are under 16 someone else in your family will be legally obliged to provide all these things for your guinea pigs and they need to agree to that!

- Do guinea pigs, from what you've learned, tick the boxes of what you'd like in a pet? If you thought they were something different don't be ashamed to change your mind. That's the whole point of finding out all about them to make the right choices.

- Can your family afford the costs you've found out? Lots of people get embarrassed talking about money but now is not the time to be shy. If you can't afford it don't get them.

- Did you have the time, energy and room to provide for all the things your imaginary pets needed? And if so, could you do that for up to eight years? If you're over the age of about 12 you may well be moving on before your guinea pigs die so your family will need to carry on where you leave off. Are they willing to do that?

- Is the whole family on board with the idea?

I hope that after all your hard work you finally get the answer you wanted but what about if you didn't? Time to ask the next question; What if the answer is no?

WHAT IF THE ANSWER IS NO?

As we said all the way back in chapter one, you should never ask yourself what sort of pet you want, you should ask yourself what sort of pet you can care for properly. The fact-finding you've done up to now will hopefully have helped you work out if guinea pigs are animals you can keep healthy and, just as importantly, happy. As I said at the end of the last chapter there is absolutely no shame in finding out the answer is no. That is the point of your mission and the book, to help you and your family make the right and responsible choice. Not only will you have happy pets but hopefully you'll have pets which make *you* happy too. Very often pets get given away because they were bought on an impulse with no research. In the case of guinea pigs it can easily happen too. If kept alone and never handled they can be very unfriendly and unhappy animals and not very nice pets through no fault of their own, simply because they are misunderstood and poorly cared for. This becomes a vicious circle, the children don't want to touch them and they get neglected or given away.

So if you have done your numbers and learnt your facts and decided that guinea pigs are not the right pet for you or your family then that is just as worthwhile as deciding to go ahead and buy some. A massive well done either way. You should be very proud of yourself. If you found that guinea pigs didn't tick your boxes or you couldn't tick theirs it doesn't necessarily mean you can't have a pet; we just need to look at some alternatives depending on what you were struggling with.

There's a brilliant animal charity called the PDSA and they've come up with a great way to think about having pets and that is to think PETS! That is Place, Exercise, Time and Spend. Going through these four things for whichever animal you are thinking about is a good way to decide if you can keep them properly. On their website they have a great tool to help people find the right pet for their own situation so do have a look at that as well. For now we'll go one step at a time through PETS and see what other pets might suit you best! Remember that this is just a pointer. You will still need to thoroughly research any pet you are thinking of. Just because one animal may need less room or be cheaper to keep there may be other things about it that might put you or your family off.

Chapter 9

Place

Guinea pigs need way more room than many people expect. We are still too used to picturing the forgotten little hutch at the bottom of the garden. You may have been very surprised to see just how much they need, especially if you fancy keeping a group of them. So here are some pet ideas that might (or might not!) be better:

Rabbits.

Rabbits can make great pets but in lots of ways are harder to keep than guinea pigs. They need quite a bit more room than guinea pigs and they too need to be kept in pairs or groups and shouldn't be kept on their own. I suspect if you didn't have room for guinea pigs then rabbits are probably best avoided as well.

Other 'small furries'.

Small furries are things like rats, mice, hamsters, and gerbils. Some of these certainly need less space than guinea pigs and would definitely be worth considering. There are some more exotic small furries kept as pets these days like chinchillas, degus and chipmunks but some of these need pretty huge cages to let them express all their behavioural needs so be very careful to do your research before you decide.

Cats and dogs.

These may be very different to what you were originally considering and in some ways need lots more space than guinea pigs but are still worth thinking about. You may have been expecting to keep your guinea pigs outside and found your garden just wasn't big enough. Maybe your house didn't have space for a large enough cage. Because cats and dogs live in the house and just go outside for fun and exercise they might actually be better for you. Both cats and dogs have very complex needs so make sure you can provide for those too.

Fish.

Fish are very calming, beautiful animals to watch and are very popular with lots of people. A fish tank will be much smaller than a guinea pig hutch and run combination but if you look into fish, always consider how much room they would like because a tiny bowl can be just as bad as a little hutch. Please, if you do look into keeping fish, find out about where they come from. Some will be taken from the wild and this could be very damaging to the place they come from.

Exercise

In the case of guinea pigs, exercise is kind of included in space because you need to give them the space and enrichment to exercise when they want to. I like to think of this 'E' as energy instead. It takes a lot of energy to care for pets properly. That energy could well be walking a dog or playing with a cat but it could also be the energy you need to keep your guinea pigs' run new and interesting. It could be the energy you need to drag yourself into a cold garden to handle, groom and play with your guinea pigs every day. If when you did your virtual month that all seemed like a lot of hassle, what else could you consider?

All pets need some commitment from you but some need less interaction or different interaction which might be easier. Rabbits will need all the same handling and care as guinea pigs when it comes to energy expenditure so are probably best avoided. Dogs in general needs lots of energy devoted to them and their exercise so if you're a bit on the lazy side steer clear of them too!

Small furries.

Some small furries like hamsters are happy not to be fussed and might quite like being left alone. Most animals will get used to being handled but not all of them really need it and might prefer not to have it if given the choice. In fact a lot of the small rodents are happy to be left alone as long as their other needs are met, like being alone or with friends and being able to behave normally. You'll still need to expend some energy looking after them but we'll look at that next.

Cats.

Cats are like teenagers; they're difficult to understand, they don't communicate well, they spend a lot of time sleeping and are likely to lash out at you for no apparent reason! Depending on the type of cat you have you'll often find that cats like to interact strictly on their own terms and will come to you when they feel like having some affection. In this way they might need less from you than guinea pigs.

Fish.

Fish might be a good alternative but make sure you know what sort of fish you are taking on and how much you will need to do to keep the environment right for them.

Time

In your virtual month, especially in the last week, you should have found that your guinea pigs need a good 1-2 hours of your time every day and sometimes more. This might not sound a lot to many people but when you actually have to do it day in and day out it can quickly become difficult to find the time. You probably won't be surprised to hear that lots of non pet detective owners don't realise the time needed until it's too late and pretty soon we're back to that neglected and forgotten hutch in the bottom of the garden or an abandoned pet.

Time is very precious to lots of people. We live in busy times. Lots of parents work, lots of kids do a million after school activities and weekends disappear in the blink of an eye. Trying to find a spare two hours every day can be a massive headache for any family, even if you share the work. All pets need some time commitment from you and it's definitely worth considering right now if you found time an issue at all in your virtual month. It's better not to have a pet than to have an unhappy, badly looked after one.

Time and energy go hand in hand. If you struggled to find the time for guinea pigs then dogs and rabbits will be the same. As we said with the small furries and cats in some ways they may need less time. It will vary depending on the animal and as always research will be important. For example if you have a longhaired cat you might need hours to try and keep its coat under control but if you end up with an independent, short haired moggie some of them pretty much look after themselves. All the small furries will need some time for cleaning and feeding and again that will vary depending on the animal and the size of their cage, how they live and how dirty they are! Fish could well be another good alternative but as with the energy required, some, like marine fish might need more time than others to keep their tank exactly right.

Time is a precious commodity, and so is money...

Spend

The cost of keeping pets is probably the most massively underestimated thing of all when it comes to owners. Stuff like bedding, toys, and cages are easy things to work out and think about but people always forget things like vets' bills and, quite shockingly, the cost of food. Feeding an animal for 2—20 years can make a big hole in your wallet!

The PDSA PAW report in 2013 asked lots and lots of owners how much they thought it would cost to look after a dog, cat or rabbit for the whole of its life. Most people thought it would cost £1000—£5000 for a dog when in fact, depending on the breed it can be up to a staggering £31,000! Most people gave the same answer of £1000—£5000 for a cat but the average is actually often a whopping £17,000. The average rabbit costs £9000 but when owners were asked what they thought it would be, nearly all of them said about £1000. As we said, guinea pigs cost roughly £2000.

You can see why people are shocked when they actually get the animals! Money is another big reason pets get given away. As I said, some people are shy when it comes to talking about money but if you're thinking of getting a pet it's absolutely vital you find out how much it is likely to cost and make sure your family can afford it. From these numbers you'll have already guessed that if guinea pigs were too much of a strain moneywise then cats, dogs and rabbits are almost certainly out of the question.

Small furries.

All the things that apply to guinea pigs also apply to most of the small furries. In general, the smaller the animal, the shorter the lifespan. For instance, a rabbit can live up to ten years, a guinea pig around five years, a hamster two years, and a mouse up to a year. Also, generally speaking, the smaller the animal, the smaller the cage you need — so on average, smaller pets should be cheaper than rabbits to keep. Some of the more exotic ones will be very different, though, so do your research.

Fish.

Fish will be really variable depending on how many and what type you have. They have hugely different needs for things like water temperature, food and care. A couple of coldwater, freshwater fish may well be cheaper than two guinea pigs but a state-of-the-art tropical underwater heaven may not!

What if You're Worried You Can't Manage Any Pet?

Above all please believe me when I say that it is better not to get a pet at all than to neglect one. Being a responsible pet owner is all about making the right choice and sometimes that means not getting one at all. Try not to be too downhearted. Look at all your options and also think about ways things might change with time. When I was very little we had no spare money at all but as we got older my mum and dad worked hard and trained and got different jobs and as time went by we found we could get a dog. Believe me I pestered for a LONG time before that actually happened!

If you have friends who have pets ask if you can spend time with their animals and help them with the jobs. You never know, they might be a bit bored with it and might love to have a helper. Just being around animals is a brilliant feeling so you might need to just take small opportunities when they come along.

Talk to your mum and dad about fostering pets. There are so many unwanted pets that lots of adoption centres often need people to foster animals while they are waiting for a home. This might mean having rabbits, guinea pigs, small furries and even dogs and cats if you can manage, but just for a short time and often with help from the charity with the costs. You'll get some animal time but will also be doing a really good deed too.

You could also find out about charities like Hearing Dogs for Deaf People. Some of the centres ask people to care for a dog in the evenings and over the weekends while it's being trained. This means if your mum and dad are at work during the day the dog just comes to you for the times you're all at home. They have lots of different volunteering options on their website so you might find something that is perfect. A temporary arrangement might be a great compromise for you and your family.

So here we are, almost at the end of your journey into the wonderful world of guinea pigs and being an A-grade owner. All that's left to say is...

Chapter 10

WELL DONE DETECTIVES!

By the time you get to here you will have worked hard and learned exactly what it takes to be an excellent pet owner. Let's think about all the amazing things you have done and achieved since page one:

* You've learnt about how animals can make us happy and what it means to be a responsible pet owner, including the serious stuff about the law!
* You've found out how wild guinea pigs live, what makes them happy and what keeps them healthy.
* You've found out what food is best for guinea pigs, which plants are safe and which are poisonous, how much food they need and how to tell if they are too fat or too thin.
* You've discovered just how much room guinea pigs need to live happily and what sort of environment will keep them safe. **A HUTCH IS NOT ENOUGH!**
* You've learnt that guinea pigs hate to be alone and need the company of other guinea pigs to feel safe, secure and surrounded by friends.
* You've found out that it's very important to let animals behave normally. Guinea pigs need to be able to play, run, popcorn, stretch out, chew, groom, graze, explore and of course eat their own poo!
* You've learnt about obesity, tooth disease, fly strike, bumblefoot, scurvy, mites and all the things you need to look out for to spot a poorly guinea pig before it gets too bad. You've also learnt that guinea pigs, because they are prey animals, don't always show pain like other animals so it's up to you to know what's normal for them.
* You've done extra research, spoken to vets and nurses, been to pet shops, looked online, done lots of maths and maybe even made your whole family sit down together to discuss this whole pet-owning business.
* Hopefully you've even gone the whole hog and made yourself feel a bit silly wandering round the garden or the house pretending to do stuff to two or more pretend guinea pigs.

Chapter 10

THAT is a very impressive list of things and that is why you should feel very proud of yourselves. I am ecstatic that you bought or borrowed this book and read it and I am very proud of you. You may feel like kids are ignored sometimes and you might feel sometimes like no-one really listens to your opinions but I'm going to let you into a secret; you kids can change the world. Let's face it, grown-ups have messed up pet keeping for hundreds of years. They think they're too busy to do research and lots of them think they know everything already!

Just imagine if you told your mum or dad all the things you'd learned about how to actually care for guinea pigs. I bet they would be astounded. I bet you could teach *them* some things. They might think it's fine to keep them on their own or with a rabbit! But now YOU know better. You might not feel like you can change the world but if all the children in the world learnt what you have and really took it on board then pet keeping would transform over night. Old, wrinkly vets like me would smile and put our feet up because our work load would halve in an instant because of all those well cared-for pets.

I've told you repeatedly that you should never ask yourself what sort of pet you want but now we're at the end of your journey I think it's time for you to do just that. You see it's very important that you ask yourself what sort of animal you can care for properly but you do also need to consider what you're looking for in a pet because you and your family need to be happy too. You might have discovered that you can perfectly care for a hundred guinea pigs but if you wanted a pet that would cuddle up on your lap every night a hundred guinea pigs might never make you happy! Owning pets is a team game so make sure you all talk about your options. If guinea pigs aren't right for you have a look at the other books in the series and keep learning. All animals are fascinating even if you don't end up with one.

If you've decided guinea pigs would make you happy and that you can keep *them* happy and healthy, hang onto the book. Unless you've got a brain the size of a planet you might want to remind yourself of things when you get your new bundles of joy. When you're deciding where to get your guinea pigs please remember adoption centres and the importance of rehoming animals. Depending on the country you live in you might find a useful website like www.guineapigfinder.com with plenty of animals looking for a loving home.

If guinea pigs now seem like the worst choice in the world then pass the book on. You could give it to a friend or sell it for some pocket money. If you've got a friend with a guinea pig you don't think is being very well looked after you could slip the book into their school bag as a nudge in the right direction. If that friend gets their guinea pig a friend, you've taken one more step towards changing the world.

At the start of the book we said that living with animals can be wonderful. I hope the books in this series will help to guide you and your family to what will be a fantastic friendship and a time that you will look back on with big smiles and a mountain of happy memories.

All that remains for me to do is to tell you again how brilliant you are and to award you with your detective certificate. Proof that you now know pretty much everything there is to know about the needs of guinea pigs.

WELL DONE!

THIS IS TO CERTIFY THAT

- -

HAS LEARNT PRETTY MUCH EVERYTHING
THERE IS TO KNOW ABOUT CARING FOR GUINEA PIGS
AND BEING AN EXCELLENT PET OWNER!

Are **Rabbits** the Right Pet for You:

Can YOU find all the facts?

Want to know what rabbits love to eat, who their friends and enemies are and what makes them happy?

You can find out by learning the facts and taking on detective assignments to investigate what rabbits need and whether you pass the test to look after them as pets.

Being a responsible pet owner is a big commitment. Rabbits, like all pets, should be looked after with care and kindness. Finding out about them before you buy your rabbits and learning all about these wonderful animals will help you be a better owner and your rabbits be happier pets.